GCSE English Language
Revise
Creative Story Writing
Model Answers and Practice
from
GCSEEnglish.uk

Edward Mooney

gcseenglish.uk

First Printing: 2023

ISBN 979-8512085905

www.gcseenglish.uk

Contents

Introduction

In this book, you will find the guidance you need to help you improve your short story writing for the GCSE English Language exams.

There are practice exam-style writing tasks, writing checklists and complete full-marks model answers to help show you what a good answer looks like and what the examiners are looking for.

The stories are very short and show what is achievable within the constraints of a timed exam.

Short story writing is a very important part of the English curriculum and represents up to 25% of your total GCSE English Language grade. Regular practice of story writing is therefore vital for boosting exam grades.

Regular story writing practice will also help boost your confidence in other forms of writing.

How to use this book

There are a range of different ways you can use this book. You could:

- read the stories and see what an excellent exam answer looks like.
- read the exam tasks and then plan and write your own stories.
- use the checklists (provided after every story) to see how many of the writing recommendations are met by each story.
- use the checklists (provided after every story) to help you plan and write your own stories.
- read the stories again, more slowly, identifying key language features (e.g. imagery, simile, metaphor, personification).
- re-write the stories from the point of view of another character or write the next chapter or a prequel to each story.

Of course, these are practice tasks and model answers. Your writing in your exam should be your own work. Don't attempt to memorise a story and copy it out as you risk being penalised, such as having marks taken away or even being disqualified from the entire exam.

More about me

I am a qualified teacher of English with a degree in English Literature from the University of Cambridge. I have taught and examined GCSE and A Level English courses at outstanding schools since 2006. I now write model answers and provide exam preparation through my website gcseenglish.uk.

Keep up to date with future projects and collections of model answers by subscribing to my newsletter or by following my social media channels. Visit gcseenglish.uk or search gcseenglishuk and feel free to leave a review.

Best of luck in your exams!

1: A story set by the sea

You are advised to spend the correct amount of time on this section (check Appendix 1 for your exam board's time).
Write in full sentences.
You are reminded of the need to plan your answer.
You should leave enough time to check your work at the end.

You are going to enter a creative writing competition.

Your entry will be judged by a panel of people of your own age.

Write a story set by the sea.

1: The Story

"You know I have to leave," said Cath, shivering into her coat as the snow fell softly into the sea. Music and laughter rang out from the bars along the seafront; everyone else was sensibly inside on this freezing New Year's Eve.

"Don't go," Onel said, turning to her. "There must be a job going for you round here?"

"I wish," said Cath. "I've been looking for ages." Two years since they'd left school and not a penny to show for it. Jobs were scarce out of season and you couldn't save up for a holiday, let alone a damp-riddled bedsit, on a candy floss seller's wage.

"Anyway, it's too good an opportunity Onel. The pay is off the scale. I *deserve* it." Best interview ever, her new boss had said.

"And," she continued, "you said yourself we've outgrown this town."

Onel kicked at the stones. It was true. He doubted if there were boarded up discount shops on Hollywood Boulevard. But it was home. "Yeah, except I love the place really. And...." He walked off, stumbling along the high tide line. The snow fell more thickly.

"Onel!" Cath tried to keep up.

"What if I leave too? The streets of London are paved with gold, right?" He spoke quickly, as the hasty decision formed in his mind. "Why don't I go and see for myself? I can..."

"Onel," said Cath, "don't do this. You know you can't leave your family. They need you."

"They need *you* too. It makes Mum's day when you come round. She hardly sees anyone since the operation."

Cath looked out over the bay, taking in the string of lights glittering along the promenade and the pier, magical now under a layer of snow. She sighed. It almost never snowed here by the sea.

"I won't forget this place. I won't forget you." She looked down. "Onel, what are you doing?" Onel was kneeling. She gasped, then laughed as the realisation sank in. She shook her head. "Onel...don't do anything you'll regret in the morning."

Onel looked up. "Cath. I should have done this years ago. Please, will you..."

"Onel!" Cath cried out and pointed down at the beach. She'd seen something. "Stop!"

"Please Cath... will you..." Onel tried again.

"Look!" Cath forced Onel to look down. He froze.

"Is that...?"

"Yes," she whispered. "Don't move."

Onel looked down at what his knees were resting on. He could just make out a lump of rusted metal, dented by years of being knocked around by thousands of tides, encrusted with limpets, a German inscription half visible under a kelp frond. It was unmistakeable.

Onel started to shiver. The bomb shifted on the shingle.

"What do we do Cath?"

"I don't know mate. But..." She looked at it, rusted and broken. "It's not going to go off, is it? After all these years?" She was tempted to give it a kick.

"Do you want to take that chance?"

"Do we have any other option?" They were beginning to shiver uncontrollably now. "If we stay here any longer, we'll be dead anyway."

Onel nodded. He held his hand out to Cath. "On three?"

Cath nodded.

"One." Onel tensed. "Two." He breathed in and saw in a moment the beauty of the town blanketed in snow and darkness. "Three."

They ran for their lives, falling and stumbling then crawling up the steep shingle beach. Then rising again and running. As they ran, the darkness exploded into light and the night into colour. They sprinted, tasting blood in their mouths, lungs bursting, and collapsed onto the promenade.

"We made it!" shouted Onel.

"Yeah!" shouted Cath. "We're going to live forever!" It was great to be alive. She looked back as the explosions continued and began to laugh as she realised what was happening.

Onel looked back too, in time to see the last of the New Year firework display. The bomb lay quietly on the beach, minding its own business, as it had done since it was dropped decades ago.

After a quick call to the police – "Yeah, this happens all the time" – they walked home arm in arm as dawn broke, laughing with relief, telling and retelling the night's events, practising how they would recount this story for the rest of their lives, Onel swearing that he wasn't just about to propose, honest.

And the sun rose over the snow dappled hills, the waking town, the grey rolling sea and the uncertain future beyond.

1: Writing Checklist

As you read, check how many of the recommendations below are followed by the story. Then, use the checklist to help you write your own story.

Remember that these are recommendations from an experienced teacher, not requirements. Allow them to help and guide you, but don't allow them to restrict you; if you have a different idea and feel confident about it, give it a go!

☐ Two main characters.

☐ Characters have names.

☐ Characters' approximate ages are suggested/stated.

☐ Characters' personalities are presented.

☐ How the characters know each other is clear.

☐ Specific place.

☐ Specific time of year and day.

☐ Specific weather.

☐ Description/suggestion of colours.

☐ Description/suggestion of sounds.

☐ Description/suggestion of tastes/smells.

☐ Starts with dialogue.

☐ Starts with a dramatic event. Continues with dramatic events.

☐ Contains an emotional turning point.

☐ Timeline is short (under 24 hours).

☐ Contains: imagery, simile, metaphor, personification.

☐ Paragraphs and sentences are varied lengths.

☐ Spelling, punctuation and grammar are accurate.

☐ 450-750 words.

☐ Narrated using past tense.

☐ Third person (unless exam task requires First Person).

☐ 'Show, don't tell' technique used widely.

2: A story about a sporting or cultural event

You are advised to spend the correct amount of time on this section (check Appendix 1 for your exam board's time).
Write in full sentences.
You are reminded of the need to plan your answer.
You should leave enough time to check your work at the end.

You are going to enter a creative writing competition.

Your entry will be judged by a panel of people of your own age.

Write a story about a sporting or cultural event.

2: The Story

"Nothing like watching the rugby in Dublin is there?" said Frank. "Pity we couldn't get tickets."

"No matter," said Dan. "This is much better than watching it at home." He took a gulp of his pint and gazed around the pub. "Alone." He thought of his house back over in England, empty and echoing.

Frank looked sidelong at his brother. He'd been a wreck since Finnoula had left. "We'll have none of that," said Frank, gently. "We're here to enjoy ourselves." He took another mouthful of his pint. "And to forget."

The band started playing the anthems but was soon drowned out by a pubful of middle-aged men bellowing in Welsh and Irish.

A few tears pricked the eyes and were quickly blinked away. For a moment, Frank and Dan were transported back to the two-room cottage that somehow managed to house all fourteen of them, to the tiny school where they'd learnt the words to the anthem and to the alcoholic terror of a teacher who rammed the Irish into their heads.

Frank placed his arm across his brother's shoulders. "Christ. Old Coughlan said we'd come to nothing," he said. "Look at us now!"

Dan shrugged his brother off his shoulders. He wasn't in the mood to celebrate. "Yeah, but we had to leave to come to something." The cottage was now a ruin. A motorway was tarmacked through the field where they used to play. The teacher was long dead. "And even then, it wasn't enough for Finnoula."

"She'll come back Dan. Just give her time," said Frank, not believing for a moment what he was saying. "Maybe another pint will cheer ye up?" he hinted.

Dan looked up and sighed. "I'll get them in," he said, heading for the bar. Frank nodded, absorbed in the game.

Dan's phone vibrated and he slid it from his pocket and read the message. It was Finnoula – a short but devastating message.

He froze and turned to look at his brother who was now talking and joking with some Wales fans, and through a fog of Guinness and despair came the cold stab of anger. And retribution.

He moved quickly, reached Frank and pushed his shoulder hard. Frank spilled the last of his pint over his front and turned in shock.

"You!" shouted Dan. "You?"

Frank's face fell. Finnoula'd cracked. He'd hoped to maintain the lie until they got home. He reached for his usual tactic, held his hands up and adopted a comic tone: "All right guvnor. It's a fair cop. I'll come quietly."

That was a miscalculation.

Dan went for him. They hadn't fought since their youth and neither was in good shape, but Dan got in a couple of solid body blows before being grabbed by the landlord. Frank backed away.

"Listen Dan. I can explain," he said, searching from the corner of his eye for the door. "She said you had grown apart." He reached the door. "She was lonely."

"Lonely, *mo thóin*," shouted Dan.

The landlord was shouting at them to get the hell out. The other drinkers looked on with interest. They were hoping for a bit of a ruck.

Dan tried to pull free. Frank ran for his life out into the street. The cold air hit him hard. He stopped and fell to his knees. Across from him, a frowning shaven-headed teenager in a Dublin GAA jersey squeezed hard at his accordion. A reel skipped and fluttered out over the heads of the passing shoppers who carefully stepped around Frank as snow began to fall from the hard grey sky.

Dan, ejected from the pub, looked at his brother. Frank looked at Dan. The old music filled the space between them and conjured images of the penniless emigrants who had gone before them, passing down this street to the quays, hopeful of a new life, never to return. The reel faded and died.

"Dan," said Frank. He held his arms out. "I'm sorry."

Dan shook his head, checked his watch, turned and headed for the ferry, looking forward to a nice bacon sanger, a cup of dark tea and the salt spray of the sea. An emigrant once again.

Frank stumbled to his feet and stood and watched his brother leave. He scrabbled in his pocket and dropped a few coins in the busker's hat. The teenager began playing Raglan Road, the snow fell with a sigh into mutinous Liffey waves and the afternoon continued as any normal Saturday in Dublin.

2: Writing Checklist

As you read, check how many of the recommendations below are followed by the story. Then, use the checklist to help you write your own story.

Remember that these are recommendations from an experienced teacher, not requirements. Allow them to help and guide you, but don't allow them to restrict you; if you have a different idea and feel confident about it, give it a go!

☐ Two main characters.

☐ Characters have names.

☐ Characters' approximate ages are suggested/stated.

☐ Characters' personalities are presented.

☐ How the characters know each other is clear.

☐ Specific place.

☐ Specific time of year and day.

☐ Specific weather.

☐ Description/suggestion of colours.

☐ Description/suggestion of sounds.

☐ Description/suggestion of tastes/smells.

☐ Starts with dialogue.

☐ Starts with a dramatic event. Continues with dramatic events.

☐ Contains an emotional turning point.

☐ Timeline is short (under 24 hours).

☐ Contains: imagery, simile, metaphor, personification.

☐ Paragraphs and sentences are varied lengths.

☐ Spelling, punctuation and grammar are accurate.

☐ 450-750 words.

☐ Narrated using past tense.

☐ Third person (unless exam task requires First Person).

☐ 'Show, don't tell' technique used widely.

3: A story about a place that is severely affected by the weather

You are advised to spend the correct amount of time on this section (check Appendix 1 for your exam board's time).
Write in full sentences.
You are reminded of the need to plan your answer.
You should leave enough time to check your work at the end.

You are going to enter a creative writing competition.

Your entry will be judged by a panel of people of your own age.

Write a story about a place that is severely affected by the weather.

3: The Story

"We'll be all right without them, won't we?" asked Delia as the rest of the team disappeared off down the road back to town. She looked up at the sky, grey from horizon to horizon. The mountains were invisible under the blanket of cloud. Fields lay under water, flooded and desperate. Sheep huddled in the lee of drystone walls, shivering.

"It's just a light drizzle," said Myleene. She shivered. "But we should probably get moving. We've got 10 miles and 920 vertical metres to cover, and time is against us. Sunset is at..." she checked her expedition planner, "...19:48."

Delia smiled. "Impressive work. Maybe the Duke of Edinburgh will present the award personally."

"If he's not there, after this ordeal, I'll demand my taxes back." Myleene could feel the rain running down the back of her neck. "And instead of a badge, how about a crown? They've got enough of them knocking around."

"Or a tiara?"

"I'd look deadly in a tiara," said Myleene. "And I've always wanted an orb and sceptre."

"Who hasn't?" Delia laughed.

They trudged and squelched onwards, up into the grey. Rucksacks bit into tired shoulders. Rain spattered the face of the compass. They were two dots, red and blue, moving slowly across the moor. Mud clung to their boots, making each footfall slower and heavier. Stiles seemed to get higher and higher. Delia fell. Myleene dragged her up. Myleene fell. She lay stranded, like an inverted turtle, face to the sky. Delia laughed as she helped her up.

Tired now and hungry, they carried on. The path became a scratch in the earth and then dwindled into invisibility.

They stopped. They were lost in a world of heather and rock and the calling and crying of a thousand mountain streams.

"We're lost," said Myleene. She looked back down the mountain. "Perhaps we should have bailed with the others after all."

"Hey. None of that talk." Delia dumped her rucksack, opened it, pulled out the stove and began heating water. "Let's have some tea and warm up and we'll think of a plan."

They sat on a groundsheet, hands around their mugs, grateful for the heat. The tea revived them, cheered them. But they still shivered.

"Why do we do this to ourselves?" asked Delia.

"I need it for my UCAS form."

"Is that it?"

Myleene shrugged. "Maybe it's all about the glory of the English landscape?" She gestured off into the fog, visibility now down to mere metres.

Delia laughed.

"I think I'm just trying to escape." Myleene spoke about the emptiness of days spent in stuffy classrooms, hours lost on the school bus stuck in traffic, evenings spent alone scrolling through Instagram, dreaming of California but waking up in Scroby. "Or, just searching for meaning like everyone."

Delia nodded. "There are easier ways to escape though. Ones that don't require Gore-Tex and toilet trowels."

Myleene smiled and drank the last of her tea. "What are you escaping from?"

Delia looked at her. "Other than the usual?"

Myleene nodded.

"Well," Delia hesitated, "until last week I thought I was pregnant." She paused. "And now I'm not."

Myleene struggled. This was too much for her. "I'm...sorry. I didn't know."

"Don't worry. Hardly anyone does. And it all happened so quickly." She spoke quietly as the rain continued: the first shock then the joy, her parents' reactions, her boyfriend's fear, and silence. A different future suddenly opened up and then came the pains and the bleeding. And it was over.

"In theory, everything's back to normal now. But," she sighed, "I don't see how it can be. And now we're lost on a mountain?"

Myleene reached out and held Delia's hand. She didn't know what to say. They sat in silence, shivering as the day waned.

"I'm sorry," said Delia. "I've made things awkward."

Myleene shook her head. "It's me, not you. I've never been very good talking about feelings." She stood up and looked out into the gloom. "Let's get off this mountain."

The wind strengthened and the clouds parted. A sunbeam pierced the mist and in a moment the valley opened before them. They gasped as they saw what was about them, encircling them in a protective embrace: concentric circles of daffodils, spreading beyond them to eternity, smiling and dancing in the late afternoon sunshine, as far as the eye could see. Light after darkness.

Delia laughed with joy.

Myleene smiled. "This way," she said. "We're safe now."

They set off.

3: Writing Checklist

As you read, check how many of the recommendations below are followed by the story. Then, use the checklist to help you write your own story.

Remember that these are recommendations from an experienced teacher, not requirements. Allow them to help and guide you, but don't allow them to restrict you; if you have a different idea and feel confident about it, give it a go!

☐ Two main characters.

☐ Characters have names.

☐ Characters' approximate ages are suggested/stated.

☐ Characters' personalities are presented.

☐ How the characters know each other is clear.

☐ Specific place.

☐ Specific time of year and day.

☐ Specific weather.

☐ Description/suggestion of colours.

☐ Description/suggestion of sounds.

☐ Description/suggestion of tastes/smells.

☐ Starts with dialogue.

☐ Starts with a dramatic event. Continues with dramatic events.

☐ Contains an emotional turning point.

☐ Timeline is short (under 24 hours).

☐ Contains: imagery, simile, metaphor, personification.

☐ Paragraphs and sentences are varied lengths.

☐ Spelling, punctuation and grammar are accurate.

☐ 450-750 words.

☐ Narrated using past tense.

☐ Third person (unless exam task requires First Person).

☐ 'Show, don't tell' technique used widely.

4: A story in which a character makes a snap decision

You are advised to spend the correct amount of time on this section (check Appendix 1 for your exam board's time).
Write in full sentences.
You are reminded of the need to plan your answer.
You should leave enough time to check your work at the end.

You are going to enter a creative writing competition.

Your entry will be judged by a panel of people of your own age.

Write a story in which a character makes a snap decision.

4: The Story

"Plans for the bank holiday Nile?" asked his supervisor as they removed overalls and hairnets at the end of another double shift.

"A few ales of course boss," said Nile, slamming his locker shut. "What about yourself?"

"I dare say a few wines shall be quaffed," she said. "And no chocolate will pass my lips, that I can tell you."

They laughed as they headed out into the fresh air but the hanging, cloying stench of cocoa butter and sucrose followed them. The workers said their goodbyes and headed home for the Easter weekend. The last lorry load of eggs sped off into the gloom.

"See you on Tuesday for advent calendars and chocolate coins," said Lisa as she cycled off. Nile nodded his goodbye.

Soon, the chocolate factory was silent, and night was falling. A helpful mist came in over the frozen furrows. Fine weather for rustlers, ne'er-do-wells and those with something to hide.

Nile shivered, waiting. He felt the fatigue from the 16-hour shift seep into the depths of his body and fought against sleep.

A message pinged on his phone: "Where's my chocolate??!?!" Then: "Miss you Dad."

He replaced the phone, message unanswered. He wondered what she'd think of her surprise.

"'Cause I've got a golden ticket!" A singing voice emerged from the shadows.

Nile jumped. "All right JD. No need to creep up like that."

"I've got a golden twinkle in my eye." JD sang and rubbed his hands. "I love a good heist. It's what keeps me going through those long nights in the cells, counting down my days until the next big job."

"This is my last job," said Nile. "I'm just doing this for my daughter and then..."

JD laughed. "Can't tell you how many times I've heard that!" He kept chuckling. "How are you justifying it to yourself then? One last job just to get a pension pay out and then it's Costa del Sol all the way? San Miguel and temping? I give it five months."

Nile sighed. He feared JD was right, but he couldn't think of any other way out, not with his record. "Let's get this over then." He showed JD the unlocked side gate that led to the weed-choked alley behind the factory. JD nodded then got to work. In only a few moments, the back loading bay was open, the alarms and CCTV cameras were disabled, and they were inside.

"Excellent." JD checked his watch. "They'll be here with the van in ten minutes. Show me where the gear is."

"Not before payment."

JD's face fell. His false jollity dropped away as he stepped close to Nile. "Are you saying you don't trust me?"

Nile winced. JD stepped even closer, pushing Nile up against the wall.

"Put it this way: you're not getting out of here without my say so. And if you want a plump brown envelope, like we discussed, so you can run off and be with your daughter or whatever sob story you want to tell the police when they inevitably catch up with you, then you'd better do as I say."

Nile nodded.

"Got it?"

Nile nodded again.

"Good." JD stepped back. "So, where's the stuff?"

Nile led him to the office where the computers were stored, still in their original boxes.

JD's eyes lit up. "Oh yes! You weren't wrong. There must be," he made a quick calculation, "two hundred here. We're going to make a killing. Come on then, give me a hand. The van will be here in a minute." He turned around but Nile was gone.

The door slammed.

"Nile! Get back here." JD pummelled the locked door. There was no answer. "Don't do this man. Don't do this." No response. He threw himself at the door, but it didn't budge. "Nile!" JD screamed. "I'll find you. I will track you down. You'll swing for this."

As Nile ran, the shouting faded. He ran down the alley, jumped the fence and made off across the fields. He felt the frost clawing at his face and his body starting to lose control to violent shivering. He stumbled, tasting iron and blood in his throat, trying to outrun his past, the people who had failed him and his many failures.

His phone pinged again – his only lifeline. He held it like a talisman to light his way.

"Just keep going till dawn," he said to himself. "Just keep going."

4: Writing Checklist

As you read, check how many of the recommendations below are followed by the story. Then, use the checklist to help you write your own story.

Remember that these are recommendations from an experienced teacher, not requirements. Allow them to help and guide you, but don't allow them to restrict you; if you have a different idea and feel confident about it, give it a go!

☐	Two main characters.	☐	Starts with dialogue.
☐	Characters have names.	☐	Starts with a dramatic event. Continues with dramatic events.
☐	Characters' approximate ages are suggested/stated.	☐	Contains an emotional turning point.
☐	Characters' personalities are presented.	☐	Timeline is short (under 24 hours).
☐	How the characters know each other is clear.	☐	Contains: imagery, simile, metaphor, personification.
☐	Specific place.	☐	Paragraphs and sentences are varied lengths.
☐	Specific time of year and day.	☐	Spelling, punctuation and grammar are accurate.
☐	Specific weather.	☐	450-750 words.
☐	Description/suggestion of colours.	☐	Narrated using past tense.
☐	Description/suggestion of sounds.	☐	Third person (unless exam task requires First Person).
☐	Description/suggestion of tastes/smells.	☐	'Show, don't tell' technique used widely.

5: A story about a time when things turned out unexpectedly

You are advised to spend the correct amount of time on this section (check Appendix 1 for your exam board's time).
Write in full sentences.
You are reminded of the need to plan your answer.
You should leave enough time to check your work at the end.

You are going to enter a creative writing competition.

Your entry will be judged by a panel of people of your own age.

Write a story about a time when things turned out unexpectedly.

5: The Story

"I knew there'd be trouble," whispered Cáit as she posed for the last wedding photo. "We'll need peacekeepers before the night is out."

"Just keep smiling," hissed Will. "We'll get through this."

The families sat divided, staring at each other. Cáit's plan to bring cultures and people together was hopelessly naive. It's still a long way from Ballinadee to Ballymena.

"Of course, in my day, we'd have sung God Save the Queen," Will's grandmother Victoria was opining as the couple sat back down. "I see we're too good for that now."

"Er…thanks nan. Always great to hear about the old days," said Will hurriedly.

Victoria harrumphed, as only a grandmother who has seen it all can, and lapsed into silence.

"We had the anthem at my wedding too," said Cáit's grandfather Tadhg, leaning across to Victoria. "Of course, it wasn't your one we were singing." He breathed in, ready to sing.

"Grandad!" cut in Cáit. "Didn't I hear you got a new car?"

"It is a tractor I got. The finest in the west. Sure, she needs a bit of twine here and there, but she'll cover an acre with muck no bother."

Cáit had her head in her hands. The cultural gap yawned wide. She'd really hoped the wedding would pass with no mention of red diesel or slurry tank agitation.

Victoria leant forward. "I remember the time we got our first tractor. Dad took us for rides up and down the land." Her hands moved in front of her, tracing the paths of her memory. "And then we learnt to drive it. We were really going places back then."

"Ah Cáit. What have you been playing at?" said Tadhg, accusation in his voice.

Cáit was taken aback. "What?"

"You never told me they were farming people." He turned to Victoria. "How many acres is it you're farming now?"

There was a sharp intake of breath. Victoria sighed. "None sadly. The bank took it off us during the...bad time." She paused. "I've never been back."

"You'll have to come down to visit. We've plenty of room and you can have a spin on the tractor. We'll give you a big feed into the bargain. How's that sound?"

"Oh, that's very kind...er...Tadhg," said Will, struggling as always with just which of the letters were silent in his name, "but I think nan's a bit too old to..."

"Who are you calling old?" Victoria said. "I survived a world war and...other troubling events. I can survive a trip on the train."

"We'll roll out the red carpet and no mistake. Now, you must have a song or two. Will you sing us one?"

Victoria was unsure. Will held his breath, desperate for her not to break out the 'send her victorious'.

"There's an old song my mother sang to us," said Victoria. "I might not know all the words."

"Give it a go. We'll help you out," said Tadhg.

Will looked at Cáit. This was not really what they had expected. By now they were supposed to be dancing to Ed Sheeran.

Victoria closed her eyes and a quiet voice, hesitant at first, called up an ancient song from deep in her past. Each word somehow expressed profound sorrow, burning anger and a capacity for hope. The last notes faded and died.

Victoria looked up and smiled at Tadhg. He smiled and snuffled away a tear or two. "Now that's a powerful song," he said. "A powerful song. I'll be hearing that one in my dreams."

"Will you give us one Tadhg?" said Will.

Tadhg's eyes lit up. "I thought you'd never ask." He stood, downed his pint of stout, and addressed the room. "Now this one's a waltz so I expect to see you all up and dancing."

Will stood, held his hand out for his wife and led her to the dancefloor as the first notes of the song began in Tadhg's bright tenor voice.

"Trasna na dtonnta, dul siar dul siar..." And Tadhg gave the song all he had. "Bright is my heart and bright is the sun..."

Cáit and Will waltzed uncertainly as they remembered the day they met and the joy that ran through them like fire through heather, a joy so sharp and beautiful it hurt.

And the notes of Tadhg's song fell like a blessing as they danced, smiling tearfully as they whispered to each other and tearfully smiling as the old song in a half-dead language faded into the summer night.

5: Writing Checklist

As you read, check how many of the recommendations below are followed by the story. Then, use the checklist to help you write your own story.

Remember that these are recommendations from an experienced teacher, not requirements. Allow them to help and guide you, but don't allow them to restrict you; if you have a different idea and feel confident about it, give it a go!

☐ Two main characters.

☐ Characters have names.

☐ Characters' approximate ages are suggested/stated.

☐ Characters' personalities are presented.

☐ How the characters know each other is clear.

☐ Specific place.

☐ Specific time of year and day.

☐ Specific weather.

☐ Description/suggestion of colours.

☐ Description/suggestion of sounds.

☐ Description/suggestion of tastes/smells.

☐ Starts with dialogue.

☐ Starts with a dramatic event. Continues with dramatic events.

☐ Contains an emotional turning point.

☐ Timeline is short (under 24 hours).

☐ Contains: imagery, simile, metaphor, personification.

☐ Paragraphs and sentences are varied lengths.

☐ Spelling, punctuation and grammar are accurate.

☐ 450-750 words.

☐ Narrated using past tense.

☐ Third person (unless exam task requires First Person).

☐ 'Show, don't tell' technique used widely.

6: A story with the title 'Abandoned'

You are advised to spend the correct amount of time on this section (check
Appendix 1 for your exam board's time).
Write in full sentences.
You are reminded of the need to plan your answer.
You should leave enough time to check your work at the end.

You are going to enter a creative writing competition.

Your entry will be judged by a panel of people of your own age.

Write a story with the title 'Abandoned'.

6: The Story

"Mate – where are you?" asked Bryan into his phone, leaving yet another voicemail message. "We said we'd meet by the cider bar." He scanned the crowd again. No sign. "Where are you?" He looked at his old friend Jez. Jez shrugged.

Around them a multitude flowed, an eddy of neon and laughter and crushed apple. Music pounded the air. Bass notes thrust up through the earth. The night was turned to an uncanny day by laser shows and festoon lights strung along the hawthorn hedgerows. Beyond the festival site, out in the midsummer darkness, grumpy villages slept fitfully, excluded from the merrymaking.

Bryan suddenly wanted to be anywhere but here.

"You don't need them," said Jez, handing Bryan a cider.

"I can't believe it," he said. "They're good friends."

"Maybe," he said, "but they were using you."

"What do you mean?" Bryan asked, but he knew Jez was right.

"Have they paid you for the tickets yet?"

Bryan shook his head and gazed at the ground. The grass was trodden down, and the earth was beaten hard. Shards of flint glimmered.

"Did they give you petrol money or thank you for organising everything?"

Bryan shook his head again.

"Have they asked you about your operation?" Jez kept probing.

Bryan threw the cider down. There was laughter from passing revellers.

Jez hesitated than asked one more question. "Did any of them visit you in hospital?"

Bryan flinched. He remembered the sense of isolation and fear during those long days. He remembered who stood by him, and who abandoned him.

"Come on," Jez said, slapping Bryan on the shoulder. "I know what'll cheer you up." He moved off through the crowd. Bryan had to run to keep up.

"Where are we going?"

"Just keep up," said Jez with a laugh. "Magical mystery tour. Just like old times."

They moved quickly. Past: pie stalls, gem therapists, tie-dye workshops, compost toilets, a tv comedian stopping for selfies, hawkers and pedlars of items legal and illegal, a drumming circle, puddles of vomit, bad guitarists, an outside broadcast crew.

Slowly the crowds thinned, the music faded. Jez slowed down. They'd reached the perimeter fence, 12 feet high, dull shimmering steel.

"You remember," he said, turning to walk along the length of the fence, "when we were young..."

"We're not old Jez," said Bryan.

"True," said Jez. "But I mean before life and jobs and bills and acrimonious break ups."

"Days of yore," said Bryan. "Climbing trees, grazed knees, staying out till dark...but we can't go back."

"Can't we?" Jez stopped. "This'll do." There was a scrabbly English oak growing near the fence. He began to climb. A branch caught and ripped his T-shirt.

"Jez, come on man. What are you doing?"

"Escaping." He looked back over the festival. "We don't need this. We can go and play out until dawn like old times, for free." He began to proclaim, arms aloft, smiling. "In fresh air, cool moonlight, supping the sweet morning dew and drinking cupfuls of dawn."

Bryan laughed. "That cider is powerful stuff."

"I didn't touch the stuff," said Jez. "I'm high on midsummer!" He kept climbing and soon was straddling the fence. "Shall we?"

Bryan looked back and realised he hadn't been enjoying himself. He'd pretended, of course, because this is what you're supposed to like. But the posing, the pretence, the emptiness of the music and the sheer amount of money sloshing about the place. No. He was done with that.

He heard an engine and saw car headlights in the distance, coming in their direction.

"Come on," said Jez. "They think they've got a gatecrasher."

Bryan clambered up the tree, grazing his knees on the ancient bark. He reached across to the fence and in one movement was up and over and falling free on the other side, into nettles skulking furtively by the other side of the fence. With a cry of pain, he dragged himself to his feet. Jez fell with a thump and jumped up.

"Let's do this," he said, and they ran as dawn broke over the ancient landscape, bringing the world to life in an explosion of butterflies and delicate summer scents. Larks sprang into the cool morning air and began their praise singing over the ripples and circles and faint marks in the land left by all those who came before. Bryan and Jez, two specks in the vastness, moved slowly east, facing the rising sun, heading home to peace and happiness and family.

6: Writing Checklist

As you read, check how many of the recommendations below are followed by the story. Then, use the checklist to help you write your own story.

Remember that these are recommendations from an experienced teacher, not requirements. Allow them to help and guide you, but don't allow them to restrict you; if you have a different idea and feel confident about it, give it a go!

- [ ] Two main characters.
- [ ] Characters have names.
- [ ] Characters' approximate ages are suggested/stated.
- [ ] Characters' personalities are presented.
- [ ] How the characters know each other is clear.
- [ ] Specific place.
- [ ] Specific time of year and day.
- [ ] Specific weather.
- [ ] Description/suggestion of colours.
- [ ] Description/suggestion of sounds.
- [ ] Description/suggestion of tastes/smells.

- [ ] Starts with dialogue.
- [ ] Starts with a dramatic event. Continues with dramatic events.
- [ ] Contains an emotional turning point.
- [ ] Timeline is short (under 24 hours).
- [ ] Contains: imagery, simile, metaphor, personification.
- [ ] Paragraphs and sentences are varied lengths.
- [ ] Spelling, punctuation and grammar are accurate.
- [ ] 450-750 words.
- [ ] Narrated using past tense.
- [ ] Third person (unless exam task requires First Person).
- [ ] 'Show, don't tell' technique used widely.

7: A story with the title 'A New Start'

You are advised to spend the correct amount of time on this section (check Appendix 1 for your exam board's time).
Write in full sentences.
You are reminded of the need to plan your answer.
You should leave enough time to check your work at the end.

You are going to enter a creative writing competition.

Your entry will be judged by a panel of people of your own age.

Write a story with the title 'A New Start'.

7: The Story

"It's coming home. It's coming home. It's coming…" The vocal fan took a deep breath, a swig from his lager and continued bellowing. "Football's coming home."

Beth tutted. "I hope it gets home soon so we can finally have some peace and quiet." She looked over at the celebrating fans that covered the beach.

They started on an exuberant rendition of a version of Guantanamera, red bellies proudly on display: "One Marcus Rashford. There's only one Marcus Rashford…."

"It's disgusting," she said. "We came here for the bracing sea air and clifftop walks and this is what we get."

Next to her, resplendent in a knotted hankie and rolled up slacks, Geoff grunted as he pumped up the paddleboard.

She made to get up. "I've half a mind to go over there and…"

"Don't," said Geoff. "Please don't. We came here without the children to relax, remember. And to…" He tailed off, unable to say the unsayable. "Give me a hand!"

The singing got louder as the crowd on the beach swelled. Herring gulls called and swooped as if joining in the celebration. Somehow, someone had got hold of a trombone and was having a pretty good go at blasting out God Save the Queen. The sun, its hat firmly on, blazed down on the fans.

A police van pulled up and disgorged its contents. There was high-vis everywhere.

"Look. I know what I did was wrong," said Geoff suddenly, staring at the horizon.

Beth looked over at him.

"I'm sorry," he said. "I thought it would solve our problems." He hung his head.

"Our problems?" asked Beth. "You mean, your problems."

Geoff nodded.

"How much?" asked Beth.

Geoff was silent. The beach was heaving now as the rising tide squeezed the crowd against the sea wall. Yet more fans joined them. A PA was rigged up and started blasting music out to sea.

"They'll be able to hear that in France," said Geoff.

"How much did you...steal?" asked Beth, enunciating each word carefully.

Geoff winced. "It wasn't stealing. Just some creative accounting. It's legal in some jurisdictions..." He kicked the paddleboard. "Come with me. We can start again. They'll never catch up with us."

Beth wondered for a moment what their new life would be like, always on the run, living on dirty money, sipping piña coladas in a tropical paradise, forever separated from the kids.

Geoff held the wetsuit out to Beth. "Just trust me. One quick trip on the paddleboard and we can be away." He looked up. A pair of police officers were walking in their direction. "Quickly," he hissed. "How'd they know I was here?" he asked himself.

"No Geoff," said Beth. She pulled the plug on the paddleboard. "It ends here. I told them." Geoff collapsed to the pebbles. "Honestly, faking your own death? Is that what it's come to?"

"A little choppy for a trip on a paddleboard wouldn't you think?" said the police officer as he placed Geoff in handcuffs. "You'd have been dead the minute you passed the harbour wall." The officers laughed.

Beth stared out over the waves as Geoff was led away. The crowd on the beach started singing The Great Escape. Fans took it in turns to be hoisted onto the crowd's shoulders and tossed into the sea. They emerged with a shout and a roar and a few cuts and bruises before joining the party again.

The crowd engulfed Beth, dancing and singing around her. "Don't worry love. You can do a lot better than that," said one fan, mini St George's flags in her hair. "What's he been arrested for anyway? Crimes against fashion." She laughed, giving Beth a slap on the back.

Beth smiled and looked up. "What was the score?" she asked.

"What was the score?" cried the fan. "Hey lads, she wants to know what the score was."

As one, they all started singing again. Beth's new friend re-lived the famous last-minute goal for her, commentating like a pro, before re-enacting the scissor kick and landing in a heap on the beach then bounding up again with a laugh.

Beth clapped.

"Hey what are you drinking? Get this woman a drink," shouted the fan.

Beth faded into the crowd as they all started singing again. The sun slid slowly from the sky and as night fell, for the first time in years, Beth danced under the stars, happy and free.

7: Writing Checklist

As you read, check how many of the recommendations below are followed by the story. Then, use the checklist to help you write your own story.

Remember that these are recommendations from an experienced teacher, not requirements. Allow them to help and guide you, but don't allow them to restrict you; if you have a different idea and feel confident about it, give it a go!

☐ Two main characters.

☐ Characters have names.

☐ Characters' approximate ages are suggested/stated.

☐ Characters' personalities are presented.

☐ How the characters know each other is clear.

☐ Specific place.

☐ Specific time of year and day.

☐ Specific weather.

☐ Description/suggestion of colours.

☐ Description/suggestion of sounds.

☐ Description/suggestion of tastes/smells.

☐ Starts with dialogue.

☐ Starts with a dramatic event. Continues with dramatic events.

☐ Contains an emotional turning point.

☐ Timeline is short (under 24 hours).

☐ Contains: imagery, simile, metaphor, personification.

☐ Paragraphs and sentences are varied lengths.

☐ Spelling, punctuation and grammar are accurate.

☐ 450-750 words.

☐ Narrated using past tense.

☐ Third person (unless exam task requires First Person).

☐ 'Show, don't tell' technique used widely.

8: A story about two people from very different backgrounds

You are advised to spend the correct amount of time on this section (check
Appendix 1 for your exam board's time).
Write in full sentences.
You are reminded of the need to plan your answer.
You should leave enough time to check your work at the end.

You are going to enter a creative writing competition.

Your entry will be judged by a panel of people of your own age.

Write a story about two people from very different backgrounds.

8: The Story

"Are you ok?" Efan linked his arm through Maggie's as she stood at the ship's railing. He gave her a cup of tea. She took it and drank gratefully.

"It's hard," she said. "I wasn't there."

Efan nodded and squeezed her arm.

"She always loved this journey." Maggie cried quietly for a while.

Smoke rose into the August sky as the ferry pushed hard against the sea, ploughing a furrow of white foam out of the blue vastness. Around them fellow passengers lounged in the sun, roasting slowly, swigging on pints of stout. Someone strummed wildly at a guitar and there was singing and laughter.

Maggie looked back and smiled. "She loved all this. She loved coming home."

Efan wasn't so sure. Brought up in the big city, he needed the noise, the smoke, the action.

They argued in the car as the roads got narrower and the villages got smaller and poorer.

"It's just false nostalgia, that's all. You don't love all this!" He gestured out at the cracked rock and bog. "You ran away from this as soon as you could. We can't come and live here. You're always saying the old farm is falling down anyway. Just a tumble of muck and rubble and half-dead cows. It'll bankrupt us!"

"But..." Maggie saw the shimmer in the cracked rock and the bright purple and glistening black of the bog. "It might save us." She looked at Efan. "And God knows we need saving."

He didn't catch her eye.

"It's not *you* though," he said. "You're all about LinkedIn and smashing your monthly sales targets and Marc Jacobs handbags. You want Dubai, Vegas, St Tropez. And..." he hesitated, "a baby." Maggie breathed in sharply. "Not this!" He gestured again, at a paddock in which a ragged donkey stood looking at a tree.

Maggie spoke with quiet intensity: "Neither of us have smashed monthly sales targets in a long time. And..." She tailed off. Her mother would have loved a grandchild running around the old place chasing after the hens. She'd struggled to hide her disappointment as false hopes were dashed repeatedly. And then she died. Now, the farm was theirs, but empty.

They drove on in silence.

The open coffin filled the room. Efan stopped dead at the threshold. He wasn't prepared for this. Maggie pushed him gently and led him to a chair.

They sat awkwardly, cups of tea perched in saucers on their knees. The old lads nursed a tot of whiskey. Occasionally, when the inspiration took them, one would walk to the head of the coffin and look down at the body. She was dressed in her finest tweeds and her Sunday shoes. A rosary had been threaded through her fingers. A sprig of wild honeysuckle had been tucked behind her ear.

The mourners whispered their goodbyes and let two or three tears fall, patting her hands and bending to kiss her forehead. They had conversations with her.

"Well, we're giving you a good send-off aren't we Mrs Farrell? They say it'll be the best funeral since old Finbarr's!"

The priest rose and said a decade of the rosary. Lips fluttered rapidly, delivering the familiar responses. Efan, head bowed, looked out of the side of his face and moved his lips silently, trying not to be too conspicuous.

"Didn't Mrs Farrell have an awful dedication to the Rosary?"

"Oh, she did." Agreement was general. "Oh, a great example to us all."

The night wore on. The tots of whiskey got larger, and tea turned into glasses of stout and at some point after eleven an accordion was produced.

Deep into the ninth verse of a seemingly endless rebel song, Efan looked around for Maggie. He downed his whiskey and made his way out into the cool night air.

He gasped and stumbled backwards. The heavens were laid out before him, a scatter, a skyscape, a soaring symphony of stars and galaxies and ancient light, like he'd never seen before in the orange skies over London.

A decision was made.

"Maggie!" He called out. "Maggie!"

Over the fields came a shout and he went towards her. She was standing, knee-deep in grass and clover, picking blackberries, singing quietly.

She turned and smiled and placed a berry between his lips. They held each other and whispered about plans and a new future and blackberry jam and how sorry they were and how happy they were.

"Will you come with me?" she asked.

"Yes, I will, yes," he said.

8: Writing Checklist

As you read, check how many of the recommendations below are followed by the story. Then, use the checklist to help you write your own story.

Remember that these are recommendations from an experienced teacher, not requirements. Allow them to help and guide you, but don't allow them to restrict you; if you have a different idea and feel confident about it, give it a go!

☐ Two main characters.

☐ Characters have names.

☐ Characters' approximate ages are suggested/stated.

☐ Characters' personalities are presented.

☐ How the characters know each other is clear.

☐ Specific place.

☐ Specific time of year and day.

☐ Specific weather.

☐ Description/suggestion of colours.

☐ Description/suggestion of sounds.

☐ Description/suggestion of tastes/smells.

☐ Starts with dialogue.

☐ Starts with a dramatic event. Continues with dramatic events.

☐ Contains an emotional turning point.

☐ Timeline is short (under 24 hours).

☐ Contains: imagery, simile, metaphor, personification.

☐ Paragraphs and sentences are varied lengths.

☐ Spelling, punctuation and grammar are accurate.

☐ 450-750 words.

☐ Narrated using past tense.

☐ Third person (unless exam task requires First Person).

☐ 'Show, don't tell' technique used widely.

9: A story set in a mountainous area

You are advised to spend the correct amount of time on this section (check Appendix 1 for your exam board's time).
Write in full sentences.
You are reminded of the need to plan your answer.
You should leave enough time to check your work at the end.

You are going to enter a creative writing competition.

Your entry will be judged by a panel of people of your own age.

Write a story set in a mountainous area.

9: The Story

"No," said Rob, looking up from the map, "we're definitely lost."

Lizzie looked out over the valley. Ravens hovered far below then swooped and spiralled out over the lake. At the head of the valley towered the spikes and spires of forbidding white peaks. The path to safety was somewhere in all this tumble of rock and ice, somewhere in this tangle of heather and bilberry bushes that reached and grabbed at ankles and left blood berry smears on their legs. She tapped her compass, but the needle swung freely. The problem was, it looked like every other valley, especially now as the sun dipped below the valley edge, bathing the mountainside with a beautiful pink glow but sending a shiver down her spine.

Night was coming.

Rob looked at her and looked down at his bare hands. He was already shivering. Lizzie knew her younger brother well. She could see the beginnings of panic in his eyes. And reproach.

"We shouldn't have come this way," he said. "We should have walked along the road like I wanted to. There's no way we would have got lost then."

"But..."

"We're freezing, tired and we ate the last food hours ago."

"But..."

He looked away from his sister and watched the last of the light fade out of the day. "We're going to die up here."

A shout rang out across the valley beneath them, and a pack of dogs howled. Hooves struck the earth and filled the dusk with their thunder.

"Come on," said Lizzie. "They've picked up the scent." She started running then looked back.

Rob was transfixed. A string of lights was moving inexorably up the mountainside, towards them. He trembled and tried to remember his half-forgotten parents. He tried to remember life before the escape, before the cataclysm, before, before... before everything changed utterly.

The memories danced and shimmered and faded like a will o' the wisp out over the cracked rock and broken earth of the mountain.

Lizzie grabbed his arm. "Come on! We've got to go now. Those horses are fast!"

But Rob had had an idea. "Fire!" He'd remembered the dark old stories his mum had told him about will o' the wisps leading unsuspecting travellers to their death.

"What?" said Lizzie, impatience and fear palpable in her voice.

Rob looked at his sister. "We need to start a fire."

"We don't have time. Anyway, you'll quickly get warm from running."

"No. Listen. There's no way we can outrun them. But," he started scrabbling around for kindling, "we can outfox them."

Lizzie looked at the line of lights drawing ever closer. He was right. There was no chance that they could run over rough ground in the dark without being caught or without tripping or breaking a limb.

"All right, all right, maybe it's a good idea," she said, "but the minute they get here and realise we aren't here, they'll just pick up the scent and keep going. It'll buy about ten minutes."

"Well, have you got a better idea?" said Rob as he struck a match and set the heather blazing.

The fire leapt from bush to bush, savage and free. The hounds howled, there was a shout and the hooves beat faster at the earth. They were closing in.

"Quick," said Lizzie. "I do have an idea."

The fire roared now, and the mountain was ablaze. Crouching and running Lizzie and Rob leapt through the scrub with agility born of months on the run. They crawled and rolled, tripped and bounced back up again. Thorns stuck into their flesh, thistles burnt battle-hardened skin, mud, deep sucking mud, threatened to swallow them whole. Yet they ran and ran back down the mountain – towards the pursuers – before throwing themselves down and holding their breath.

They lay, faces flat to the earth, silent and unseen, as the pursuers passed within metres of them.

Moments later, Lizzie and Rob were up and running again.

By dawn, they were miles away. Their pursuers were never seen again. But, they knew there would always be new pursuers. They would never give up.

A beautiful spring day sun rose, and the day was fresh and new. Rob was already asleep. Lizzie looked out one last time from the ditch where they were hiding. The coast was clear. She felt the sun warm her skin and she smiled. Then, she curled up beside her brother, took his hand and fell soundly asleep.

They were safe. For now.

9: Writing Checklist

As you read, check how many of the recommendations below are followed by the story. Then, use the checklist to help you write your own story.

Remember that these are recommendations from an experienced teacher, not requirements. Allow them to help and guide you, but don't allow them to restrict you; if you have a different idea and feel confident about it, give it a go!

☐ Two main characters.

☐ Characters have names.

☐ Characters' approximate ages are suggested/stated.

☐ Characters' personalities are presented.

☐ How the characters know each other is clear.

☐ Specific place.

☐ Specific time of year and day.

☐ Specific weather.

☐ Description/suggestion of colours.

☐ Description/suggestion of sounds.

☐ Description/suggestion of tastes/smells.

☐ Starts with dialogue.

☐ Starts with a dramatic event. Continues with dramatic events.

☐ Contains an emotional turning point.

☐ Timeline is short (under 24 hours).

☐ Contains: imagery, simile, metaphor, personification.

☐ Paragraphs and sentences are varied lengths.

☐ Spelling, punctuation and grammar are accurate.

☐ 450-750 words.

☐ Narrated using past tense.

☐ Third person (unless exam task requires First Person).

☐ 'Show, don't tell' technique used widely.

10: A story about a game that goes badly wrong

You are advised to spend the correct amount of time on this section (check Appendix 1 for your exam board's time).
Write in full sentences.
You are reminded of the need to plan your answer.
You should leave enough time to check your work at the end.

You are going to enter a creative writing competition.

Your entry will be judged by a panel of people of your own age.

Write a story about a game that goes badly wrong.

10: The Story

"Do you think we've gone too far this time?" asked Pablo, nervous as the darkness of the October evening grew thicker about them. The fog that hadn't lifted all day fell heavily now among the gravestones, its tendrils probing and seeking among the gargoyles and grotesques, enveloping them in its choking embrace.

"Pete deserves it, remember," said Anna as she dug into the cloying clay of the graveyard. "Come on," she said, looking at Pablo standing motionless, "get digging."

Pablo dutifully started digging. Anna's idea to dress up as 'Gothic gravediggers' for Hallowe'en had meant his dad hadn't batted an eyelid when he'd asked to borrow the shovel which he now sliced into the earth, hoping not to dig up any bones.

Calls and cries, howls and ghostly chanting filled the night as people gathered for the procession. On the village green, the fair was doing a roaring trade in toffee apples, candy floss and trips through the house of horrors.

"Ready?" asked Anna.

Pablo gulped. This was the bit he wasn't sure about. "Can't we just hide behind the tomb and jump out. That'll get him back for last year."

"Come on Pablo. No way he's falling for that. It's this plan or nothing." She gestured towards the grave. "What's it to be?"

Pablo thought back to last year and the nasty trick Pete had played on them and the campaign of bullying and taunting since then. He thought of the days off school Anna took, unable to face him. They'd grown up in the village together and had always played tricks at Hallowe'en. In recent years though, the tricks had taken a darker turn. Pablo still shuddered as he remembered realising, late, too late, what Pete had planned for Anna.

A branch cracked. Pablo snapped back into the present. They heard footsteps and a familiar taunting shout: "Come out, come out. Wherever you are!"

"Quick!" said Anna. "He's coming."

Pablo nodded and got into the grave. Anna covered the hole with branches and leaves and tip-toed behind the ancient yew that overlooked the churchyard.

They waited. The footsteps came closer shuffling through dead leaves.

"Anna?" said Pete. His voice was close now. "Why don't you just admit you're into me? We can stop all these stupid games."

No answer.

"I'll take you for a ride in the new Porsche I just got for my birthday." He jangled the keys. "It's pretty nippy."

He stopped, on the lip of the grave. Pablo could hear him breathing. He readied himself for the signal.

"I get it," he called out. "You want a taste of the big time. Instead of hanging around with that loser Pablo."

Pablo felt his phone buzz in his pocket, and he put the plan into action. He launched himself from the grave, doing his best impression of a zombie, groaning and moaning, sending branches and earth flying. He grasped at Pete and, before he was able to respond, Pablo had tipped him into the grave.

Pete screamed. He landed badly, his leg bent beneath him. "What the hell?" Pete called out from the grave, fear palpable in his voice.

Anna approached with her shovel and began pushing the earth into the grave. Pete called out in desperation, spitting earth from his mouth. Anna just laughed. And laughed.

Pablo grabbed her arm. "Stop," he hissed. "You've made your point." He looked around. "Let's go before anyone works out where we've gone."

Anna jerked herself free and kept shovelling. Then, in the earth she spotted something. She reached to pick it up and held it to the sky. The moon, shining weakly through the dissipating fog, reflected dully against the car keys.

"I've got a better idea," said Anna. She threw the shovel down. Pete cried out again. "Ever had a ride in a Porsche?" she asked, eyes glinting.

They left the graveyard, found the car and took it for a spin through the night, now gloriously moonlit and magical. They laughed and sang, and Pablo tried to shake off the image of Anna half-burying someone alive and hoped they'd forget about it as they made new memories.

Back in the cemetery, Pete dragged himself from the grave and limped painfully home, already planning his revenge.

10: Writing Checklist

As you read, check how many of the recommendations below are followed by the story. Then, use the checklist to help you write your own story.

Remember that these are recommendations from an experienced teacher, not requirements. Allow them to help and guide you, but don't allow them to restrict you; if you have a different idea and feel confident about it, give it a go!

☐ Two main characters.

☐ Characters have names.

☐ Characters' approximate ages are suggested/stated.

☐ Characters' personalities are presented.

☐ How the characters know each other is clear.

☐ Specific place.

☐ Specific time of year and day.

☐ Specific weather.

☐ Description/suggestion of colours.

☐ Description/suggestion of sounds.

☐ Description/suggestion of tastes/smells.

☐ Starts with dialogue.

☐ Starts with a dramatic event. Continues with dramatic events.

☐ Contains an emotional turning point.

☐ Timeline is short (under 24 hours).

☐ Contains: imagery, simile, metaphor, personification.

☐ Paragraphs and sentences are varied lengths.

☐ Spelling, punctuation and grammar are accurate.

☐ 450-750 words.

☐ Narrated using past tense.

☐ Third person (unless exam task requires First Person).

☐ 'Show, don't tell' technique used widely.

11: A story about an escape

You are advised to spend the correct amount of time on this section (check Appendix 1 for your exam board's time).
Write in full sentences.
You are reminded of the need to plan your answer.
You should leave enough time to check your work at the end.

You are going to enter a creative writing competition.

Your entry will be judged by a panel of people of your own age.

Write a story about an escape.

11: The Story

"Keep your head down," whispered Teemu as they passed through the monumental station entrance, trying not to attract the attention of the jittery conscripts guarding the way with fixed bayonets. Behind them, what seemed like the whole city was shuffling in line: cold, desperate, angry.

Edie took one last look at the beautiful murals that rose above them in the archway. They soared, full of hope and aspirations to unity, echoes of the joyful era in which they were painted, but tainted now by a thick veneer of pollution and the knowledge that the president who commissioned them was lounging in comfortable exile, most of the national wealth squirrelled away into shell corporations and Swiss bank accounts, as the nation he robbed fell into chaos and anger.

She looked up beyond them to the sky and the familiar skyline, orange now with the first lights of evening and white with the first snowfall of winter. She breathed in one last memory of home, before wrapping her greatcoat around her swollen belly and averting her gaze. She felt Teemu's hand press hers.

A train whistle cut the night and the train pulled slowly away from the platform and faded into the darkness. The crowd around them surged. People cried out. There was only one train left.

"Your papers," a conscript barked at them, his hand out.

Teemu pressed the freshly forged emigration permits into the soldier's hand, along with a carefully folded wad of banknotes.

The conscript made a good show of checking the documents before, with a flick of his fingers, demanding more money.

"The currency's crashed even more since this morning," he hissed. "This won't buy bread for more than a couple of days." He looked over their heads to the column of refugees, all desperate to leave the city of their birth. "At least you get to leave. You know what they'll do to me when the game is up."

Teemu nodded and slipped another wad of notes into his hand.

"All correct here. Pass along now. Safe journey to you," said the conscript, loudly, for the benefit of his commanding officer.

"Thank you," said Edie.

The conscript nodded. They passed onto the platform.

Doors were being slammed along the length of the train. The carriages were packed. People hung from the doorways and clambered onto the roof, despite the best efforts of the station staff to stop them.

Teemu wept.

"We're doing the right thing," said Edie. "A better life for the little one and...," she hesitated as she knew how hard it would be, "for us. And when it's all over..."

"...don't..."

"...we'll come back to the old place, sing the old songs, swim again in the river..." She tailed off. She knew she was weaving a pleasing fiction. A lot of hard truth lay ahead of them before they could ever hope to return.

An explosion lit up the sky. Faces were etched in a last moment of agony before being plunged into darkness. The soldiers starting firing, indiscriminately, into the crowd. More explosions ripped the night and the station gateway collapsed, rubble and concrete and steel, blood and life and hope.

The train started moving.

"Come," said Teemu. He grabbed Edie's hand and pulled her towards the train.

"What about you?"

"Don't worry about me." He scanned the roof of the train. "I'll try to get up there."

Hands reached out from the last carriage, urging her to leap and jump. She launched herself towards the train just as it passed the end of the platform.

Another explosion sent everyone to the ground. Teemu crouched as rubble rained down on him. The train picked up speed.

"Teemu!" Edie cried. "Run!"

It was too late. Teemu clutched his head, blood pouring to the ground, watching the train, watching his life, slide out of view. He summoned up the last of his energy.

"You're free Edie," he called out in joy and despair. "Nothing matters, Edie, when you're free."

Edie looked back and called out, but her words did not carry. The train slid silently into the tunnel.

"Look after the little one." Teemu spoke into the silence.

Snow dusted the cobbles.

Later, when an eerie, tense quiet had descended on the city, Teemu dragged himself up, turned around and braced himself to face his future, alone and scared.

11: Writing Checklist

As you read, check how many of the recommendations below are followed by the story. Then, use the checklist to help you write your own story.

Remember that these are recommendations from an experienced teacher, not requirements. Allow them to help and guide you, but don't allow them to restrict you; if you have a different idea and feel confident about it, give it a go!

☐ Two main characters.

☐ Characters have names.

☐ Characters' approximate ages are suggested/stated.

☐ Characters' personalities are presented.

☐ How the characters know each other is clear.

☐ Specific place.

☐ Specific time of year and day.

☐ Specific weather.

☐ Description/suggestion of colours.

☐ Description/suggestion of sounds.

☐ Description/suggestion of tastes/smells.

☐ Starts with dialogue.

☐ Starts with a dramatic event. Continues with dramatic events.

☐ Contains an emotional turning point.

☐ Timeline is short (under 24 hours).

☐ Contains: imagery, simile, metaphor, personification.

☐ Paragraphs and sentences are varied lengths.

☐ Spelling, punctuation and grammar are accurate.

☐ 450-750 words.

☐ Narrated using past tense.

☐ Third person (unless exam task requires First Person).

☐ 'Show, don't tell' technique used widely.

12: A story about a difficult journey

You are advised to spend the correct amount of time on this section (check
Appendix 1 for your exam board's time).
Write in full sentences.
You are reminded of the need to plan your answer.
You should leave enough time to check your work at the end.

You are going to enter a creative writing competition.

Your entry will be judged by a panel of people of your own age.

Write a story about a difficult journey.

12: The Story

"I can't," whispered Julia as she collapsed back into her wheelchair. She lay her head back and closed her eyes. "I can't."

"Yes you can Mum. I know you can," said Mark, taking her hand.

"Just leave me be," she said, breathing deeply. "Go off and enjoy your Christmas."

"We'll enjoy it a lot more with you back home. The girls want to see their Nana again."

Julia breathed deeply and smiled.

"Ready? One, two, three...now!" And she was up, standing, wobbling, almost falling, then standing again. She leant on Mark, and he realised just how light she was. She was fading away.

"We need to get you back home Mum. Get some spuds and butter into you."

Julia smiled. "A cup of tea would be nice."

A nurse busied himself sorting out all the tubes and making sure they wouldn't snag on anything, and they were off. They walked with stately slowness out of the treatment bay and down towards the ward exit. As they passed the nurses' station, there was a cheer and a small round of applause.

"This must be how the Queen feels," said Julia. She tried a regal wave and almost fell.

"No sudden movements Mum," said Mark, just about managing to keep her upright.

They entered the main corridor, long, green, echoing. They had to dodge beds, food service trolleys and rushing staff as well as all the other relatives, lost and dazed, weeping under fluorescent bulbs.

"How long have I been here son?" said Julia as they inched their way along.

"Three weeks." The worst three weeks of his life.

"What happened?"

Mark told the story again, as he did every day, about her collapse at the church and the panicking priest who found her and the mad dash down the motorway and the operations. He'd got quite good at telling it now, knew what little details to highlight, which ones the gloss over. She touched her fingers to her head and felt delicately around the tube drilled into her brain.

"I could have been a goner."

"You could."

"But I'm here."

"You are." Mark squeezed her hand.

She fell silent. They'd got into a rhythm now and were making good time. Mark could see the main entrance ahead.

"Poor Father Pat. He got a fright. I'll say a few prayers for him."

"He's been saying prayers for *you*. The Mass cards came in from all over."

Julia stopped. "From all over?"

"Yes."

"Even from..."

"Yes."

Julia looked at Mark for the first time. "I was too hard on her."

Mark hesitated. "Yes Mum. You were."

Julia started walking again. "Well, are we going to get this fresh air or not?"

They arrived at the main entrance. The lights were bright and there was noise, movement and life. A huge Christmas tree, adorned with tinsel and fairy lights, almost engulfed the reception desk. In the café, the coffee machine spurted and sent its dark caffeine aroma into the air. From the canteen came the unmistakeable smells of the same Christmas lunch they'd been serving for weeks. By the doors, charity carol singers were halfway through a dramatic rendition of Hark! the Herald, complete with enthusiastic trumpet. A baby screamed.

Julia stood in awe and shock, her gaze darting from one thing to another, trying to take it all in.

Then, the doors slid back and an icy wind, fresh from the frozen fens, heavy with the smell of earth and the dying leaves of autumn, swirled into the foyer. Against his body Mark felt his mother relax. She breathed in deeply.

"Beautiful," she whispered. She stepped forward. Lamps glowed in the winter fog. Plumes from the incinerator rose into the sky, red lights blinking atop the chimneys. Smokers huddled against the hospital wall, dragging guiltily on cigarettes.

Mark sat her down. "Tea?"

Julia's eyes lit up. "Yes please."

Mark headed back inside and nodded to his aunt as he passed.

She stepped forward, uncertain, afraid. "Julia," she said.

Julia's head whipped around to see who was talking.

"It's me."

Julia held out her hand to her sister. "Ethel."

They sat quietly, drinking tea as the light faded, talking about the good and bad old times and planning for a new future. The carol singers launched into In Dulci Jubilo and Mark stood back and let the sisters say what needed to be said.

He realised, for the first time in weeks, he was crying.

12: Writing Checklist

As you read, check how many of the recommendations below are followed by the story. Then, use the checklist to help you write your own story.

Remember that these are recommendations from an experienced teacher, not requirements. Allow them to help and guide you, but don't allow them to restrict you; if you have a different idea and feel confident about it, give it a go!

- ☐ Two main characters.

- ☐ Characters have names.

- ☐ Characters' approximate ages are suggested/stated.

- ☐ Characters' personalities are presented.

- ☐ How the characters know each other is clear.

- ☐ Specific place.

- ☐ Specific time of year and day.

- ☐ Specific weather.

- ☐ Description/suggestion of colours.

- ☐ Description/suggestion of sounds.

- ☐ Description/suggestion of tastes/smells.

- ☐ Starts with dialogue.

- ☐ Starts with a dramatic event. Continues with dramatic events.

- ☐ Contains an emotional turning point.

- ☐ Timeline is short (under 24 hours).

- ☐ Contains: imagery, simile, metaphor, personification.

- ☐ Paragraphs and sentences are varied lengths.

- ☐ Spelling, punctuation and grammar are accurate.

- ☐ 450-750 words.

- ☐ Narrated using past tense.

- ☐ Third person (unless exam task requires First Person).

- ☐ 'Show, don't tell' technique used widely.

Appendix 1: Exam Board Information

The below information is correct as of summer 2023. However, please check carefully with your exam provider as exam boards make regular changes to exam timings, marks allocations, weightings, syllabus codes etc.

Exam Board	Paper/Section	Time Allowed	Marks (%)
AQA (8700)	Paper 1 Section B (8700/1)	45 mins	40 marks (25%)
Edexcel GCSE (1EN0)	Paper 1 Section B (1EN0/01)	45 mins	40 marks (25%)
OCR (J351)	Component 02 Section B (J351/02)	60 mins	40 marks (25%)
WJEC Eduqas	Component 1 Section B	45 mins	40 marks (25%)

Appendix 2: What the examiners are looking for

GCSE exam boards will assess your writing against two Assessment Objectives:

AO5	Communicate clearly, effectively and imaginatively, selecting and adapting tone, style and register for different forms, purposes and audiences. Organise information and ideas, using structural and grammatical features to support coherence and cohesion of texts.
AO6	Candidates must use a range of vocabulary and sentence structures for clarity, purpose and effect, with accurate spelling and punctuation.

This exam board language, however, can feel a bit vague. After all, what does "coherence and cohesion" mean? Who decides what is "effective" and what isn't?

It is possible to answer those questions:

- Coherence means that your text should make sense as a whole, meaning the reader should understand clearly what's going on.
- Cohesion means your sentences should follow the expected rules and conventions of written Standard English grammar.
- It is your examiner, ultimately, who will decide what is effective and what isn't.

However, rather than answering these questions theoretically and hypothetically, the stories in this book aim to show in practical terms how it's possible to give your examiner what they are looking for, within the time constraints of the exam, whilst also showing off the full range of your creativity and writing technique.

What makes the stories in this book excellent exam answers?

The twelve stories in this book show how you can make good decisions about tone, style and register in order to write a text in the required form: a short story. The stories interweave complex characterisation, dramatic action and expressive description to create effective and imaginative stories that examiners would reward with high marks.

The stories also showcase accurate spelling, consistent punctuation, clear grammar and varied sentence structures.

Moreover, these stories are short – no more than 750 words. The first drafts were written under the same conditions as the ones you will face and therefore reflect what is possible in such a short time.

This makes them very different from most published short stories which rarely dip below 1000 words and are often much longer. These stories then are much closer in style and content to the sorts of stories you will need to write in your exam.

That's not to say nothing can be learned from reading longer short stories. In fact, some of the most powerful fiction comes in short story form so I include a list of suggested short story anthologies in Appendix 3.

Appendix 3: Suggested Further Reading

There are many different ways to write short stories and many different possible subjects. If you are interested in exploring more of the huge range of styles and topics the short story form offers, take some time before your exam to read stories written by a wide range of writers.

Two great free resources for more short stories are the award archives of the BBC National Short Story Award and The Commonwealth Short Story Prize.

There are also many excellent short story collections. Some recent published anthologies are listed below.

Happy reading!

The Penguin Book of the British Short Story 1: From Daniel Defoe to John Buchan (ISBN: 978-0141396002)

The Penguin Book of the British Short Story 2: From P.G. Wodehouse to Zadie Smith (ISBN: 978-0141396026)

That Glimpse of Truth: The 100 Finest Short Stories Ever Written (ISBN: 978-1784080051)

The Time Traveller's Almanac: 100 Stories Brought to You From the Future (ISBN: 978-1800249707)

The Art of the Glimpse: 100 Irish Short Stories (ISBN: 978-1788548809)

Stories of Ourselves: Volume One (ISBN: 978-1108462297)

Stories of Ourselves: Volume Two (ISBN: 978-1108436199)

Printed in Great Britain
by Amazon

47494860R00046